Sunshine in the Shadows

Pat Lomax

*"May the God of hope fill you with all
joy and peace as you trust in him ..."*
Romans 15:13

Production by Creative Plus Publishing Ltd.

Published and distributed by TLM Trading Limited
www.tlmtrading.com

Profits from the sale of this book go to support the
work of The Leprosy Mission in hospitals and rehabilitation
workshops abroad.

Printed and bound in Singapore by Imago

ISBN 978-0-902731-87-5

I have always enjoyed taking photographs but
at a time when I developed M.E. following a bad
viral infection, it was something that, on good
days, I could still do. Because I couldn't venture
very far, I began to look more carefully at what
was around me. The more I looked, the more I
found! Some of the photos in this book were
taken at that time, others subsequently.

In those days, concentration was also limited
but short pieces of writing would often bring
encouragement. I always hoped that one day,
I too would have something to share with
others to cheer and encourage.

I have called this book, 'Sunshine in the Shadows'
for I have found that even in the tough times,
when one reaches out to God, He responds
with blessing in some way. I pray that you will
find a blessing somewhere in these pages just
as God spoke to my own heart.

Without the help of Angela Garry this
book may never have been completed and it certainly
wouldn't have come in the form it has. She has used her
artistry and creativity with meticulous care to blend the
words and photographs with loveliness.
Thank you Angela!

I would also like to thank Kenneth Steven
for his comments and encouragement.

Sunshine and shadow, joy and pain so often lie close to one another.

Lord, if I am in the sunshine, by Your Spirit, help me to be aware of someone in the shadow; ready to feel their pain. May Your love in my heart bring warmth and cheer.

Lord, when I am in the shadow, come close, take my hand and draw me up. Let me feel Your love. Thank You for the warmth of those who care and pray.

Help me to keep praising with a thankful heart, even when it isn't easy, for I know that through that You will bring victory.

Rainbows are special to many people. This particular one is special to me. One day, after being ill for a long time, I was well enough to drive a short distance from home. I had taken my camera with me and prayed that God would help me find a photograph that would bless a great many people. It was a dull day and it began to drizzle. Not a promising start! I stopped in a lay-by and pulled out my flask of coffee but when the drizzle turned to rain I groaned. Finally, I set off again assuming there wasn't much hope of any kind of interesting photography for that day. Suddenly, the rain stopped and this wonderful rainbow appeared! I jumped out of the car and clicked away with great joy.

This photograph and others taken at the same time have been sent from one end of the world to the other. I have come to know that they have been a source of pleasure, hope and encouragement to many people.

The rainbow reminds us of God's promises. He promises eternal life to those who believe in Him (see John 3:16) and guidance throughout our lives, as we truly trust Him.

"Trust in the LORD with all your heart,
And lean not on your own understanding;
In all your ways acknowledge Him,
And He shall direct your paths." Proverbs 3:5-6 NKJV

One snowy day in the garden, I noticed these lovely Hellebores, heads bowed down, almost buried in the snow. Gently, I cleared away the snow and ice to capture their loveliness.

See the beauty of their creation.

It may be you are bowed down with everything life has flung at you, your spirit almost frozen. But if you let God in, He will gently clear away the snow and ice.

Even if suffering comes, God can take it in His hands and use it to let something of Himself glow through your life to others.

"Why are you downcast, O my soul? Why so disturbed within me? Put your hope in God, for I will yet praise him, my Saviour and my God. ..." Psalm 42:5-6

I really thought I had messed up this one completely. The dozen or so snowdrops had been beautiful and to add to my collection of images of flowers in ice, I had frozen them in water, then scanned the ice-block into my computer. The result looked a complete mess. I was just about to scrap it when I felt God say, 'Just look at what you have.' So I had another look and saw in a corner this lovely impressionistic image.

To have really shown the beauty of the snowdrops, though, I would have had to be down my knees where they grew. It came to me that, perhaps I can give others an impression of Christ, but to really show Him as He is, I have to be in that place of humility, truly taking in all He is and says.

As I have shared my thoughts about this picture, I know others have been blessed. In the real messes of life, God is ready to rescue us too. So be encouraged, if you feel your life is in a mess, tell God all about it and ask for His help. Things may change completely or He may whisper, 'Just look at what you have.' We may have more than we think and who knows what a blessing it may be to others. (See John 6:5-12)

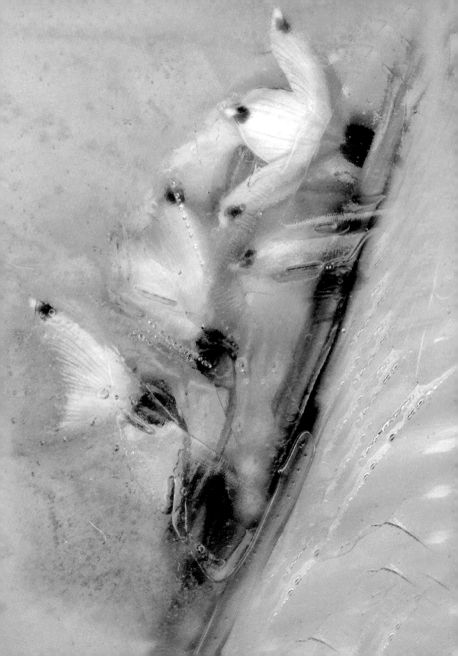

In a little crevice they grew.
Tiny poppies
Struggling to survive.
Their soil was sparse, the raindrops few.

I plucked them from their little nook.
Fragile flowers,
They soon might die I knew.
Their soil was sparse, they had no root.

Now see the deepness of their glow.
Such loveliness.
Bolder counterparts forgotten,
These still bring joy to all I know.

In a little crack perhaps you grow,
Feeling small,
Life's joy now stemmed.
Your soil is sparse, your teardrops flow.

But God can take you in His hand,
So kind and strong,
To make a rich and vibrant life.
His soil is good, with Him you'll stand.

C

lover hiding rabbits snuggled
in their petal wraps.

A single clover flower seemed particularly
lovely as I walked past a patch of clover one
day. Looking more closely I saw what, to me,
resembled rabbits wrapped like a bouquet of
flowers. Others say they see angel wings.
On a deeper level, however, it triggered
off the following verse:

"I will give you the treasures of darkness
And hidden riches of secret places...
I have even called you by your name;
I have named you, though you have not known Me."
Isaiah 45:3-4 NKJV

In looking up the context of these words, I
discovered that, not only were they spoken to
Cyrus, a heathen Persian king, but they were
spoken about 160 years before he was born!
God had plans to use Cyrus and promised
him hidden treasure.

Clover

What seemed totally impossible happened. This is an interesting, historically documented, story that is worth researching. God knows all about us! He has plans for our lives and there is 'treasure' waiting to be found for those willing to co-operate with Him. No matter how impossible something may seem, if it is His will, then with God it is possible.

Blueberries lie like tiny ceramic bowls glazed in a potter's workshop.

This made me think of a potter's workshop that one day, many years ago, had a visit from a prophet. As Jeremiah watched the potter at work, he noticed that when a pot turned out badly, the potter would sometimes take the clay and reshape it into another pot.

One of the key points of the message he was given was, that for those who repent and are willing to go His way, God will take the broken mess of their lives and make a completely new creation. In this way, something lovely, useful and pleasing to Him can be made. We become:

"...God's workmanship, created in Christ Jesus to do good works, which God prepared in advance for us to do." Ephesians 2:10

Blueberries

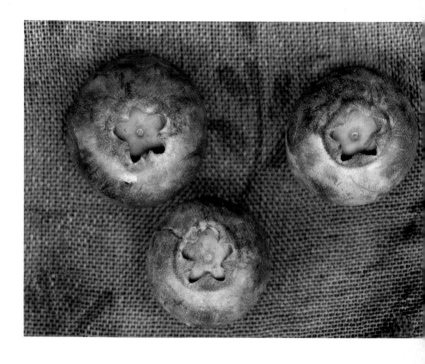

"*Go down to the potter's house, and there I will give you my message.*" Jeremiah 18 : 2

Lavender waved wildly in the wind. A very busy bumble bee with red pollen baskets on its legs caught my eye. Patience was required for this shot. The bee also required patience. Back and back it came, gathering the fine dust that was pollen. Using its combs and brushes, it filled its baskets. Those fine grains of pollen would be a good source of protein for its family. Not all the dust would reach the baskets, however. Some would brush off onto the next floret to be used in reproduction; each grain important.

Even smaller than pollen grains are the marine diatoms that I find so fascinating. They are a type of plankton and so small that apparently about 25 million of them would fit into a teaspoon! They produce at least a quarter of the oxygen that we breathe and provide nutrition to huge whales. If they escape the whales, their bodies eventually fall to the ocean floor and, in time, become petroleum. Their silica shells are mined for use as abrasives and filters. Yet each individual shell, seen under the electron microscope, is incredibly beautiful!

Feeling small? Take courage. Jesus said:

"Are not five sparrows sold for two pennies? Yet not one of them is forgotten by God ... Don't be afraid; you are worth more than many sparrows." Luke 12:6-7

Year after year, the Rhododendron bush in my garden brings me great joy. It is just an ordinary Rhododendron bush but taking a closer look one day,

> A haunting beauty met my eyes.
> Carpel and Stamens rose,
> poised in graceful elegance
> on their royal stage,
> waiting for the music of the wind
> to begin their dance.

Closer acquaintance with people too, can often reveal an unexpected hidden beauty.

I think also of the apostle Paul, the one-time hater of Jesus Christ, who was changed so dramatically by an encounter with Him that he could say:

"... I consider everything a loss compared to the surpassing greatness of knowing Christ Jesus ..."
Philippians 3 : 8

Buttercups splashed across a field
    bring memories of times we filled
    our mother's blue glass bowl
with shining golden flowers.
How good they looked against the blue.

With siblings many years before
she too had roamed the fields
to find such treasure.
They'd stop to hold them under chins.
A crucial test; they all liked butter!

Home they would go with aprons filled
to see their mother's great delight
when on the old scrubbed table
they would set
a bowl of gleaming gold.

*"And why do you worry about clothes? See how
the lilies of the field grow. They do not labour or
spin. Yet I tell you that not even Solomon in all his
splendour was dressed like one of these. If that is
how God clothes the grass of the field, ...will he
not much more clothe you, O you of little faith?*

So do not worry, saying, 'What shall we eat?' or
'What shall we drink?' or 'What shall we wear?' ...
your heavenly Father knows that you need them.
But seek first his kingdom and his righteousness,
and all these things will be given to you as well."
Matthew 6:28-33

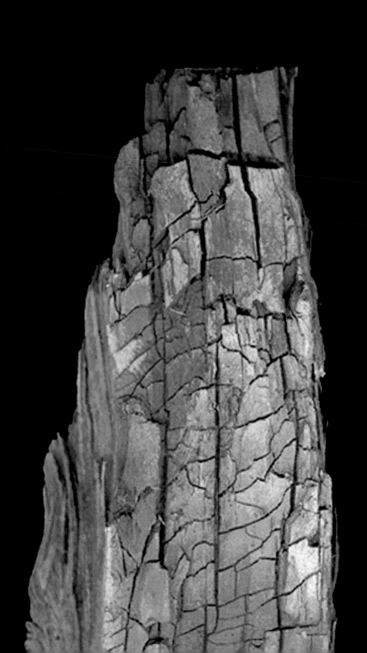

Woods can be a constant source of delight through all the seasons of the year. Even on a miserable day, like this one was, it is possible to find hidden treasure.

Going over to an old broken tree, I noticed the lovely pattern and warm colour of the wood. Nearby was a fallen birch, and even in its deterioration an interesting variety of patterns had formed. Some of the bark was like parchment.

This piece particularly thrills me when I see the deep glow. At the top there is a cross. It reminds me of someone whose life has perhaps been hard, but because of the cross a glow like a fire is coming from deep within.

Lord, may Your cross become ever more meaningful to me and Your life glow more greatly from within me.

"Say among the nations, 'The LORD reigns...'
...Then all the trees of the woods will rejoice...."

Psalm 96 : 10, 12 NKJV

My watch had stopped and by the time I discovered that my living room clock was three quarters of an hour slow, it was too late to go to church. So it was morning worship in the woods with the birds for a choir. How they sang!

The old gnarled tree stood there with up stretched arms. Sap, drawn up from roots that went deep, had surged upwards causing new life to burst out. Oh God, Creator of life, Creator of new life, how great You are! How wonderful that that old tree, which has stood there barren all winter, is now bursting with new life. Only You could do that.

'How great He is. How great He is.'
Even the chaffinch is singing it. Little chaffinch, I see you. You are beautiful. He made you too. Lord, that little chaffinch is so lovely.

Down through the beech woods, spacious and lovely.
My heart is praising. Tall larch trees sway in the breeze.
How green they look against that blue sky. What a
vastness up there! Lord of creation, how wonderful it
all is. What an amazing God you are. Look at those
white clouds moving slowly across that deep blue.
How majestic they are.

» » » »

« « « A buzzard glides past and flies off into the
distance, the black tips clearly seen on
its powerful wings. Two colourful
jays fly out of the trees calling
noisily as they go, a pheasant
croaks in the distance and oystercatchers cry
and wheel around flashing white in the sun.
What a joy, Lord.

Sitting on a tree stump eating my lunch:
Lord, this bread tastes so good. I can just
see in my mind a field of golden wheat with
the wind rippling thorough it.

Thank You for the wheat, for the rain that
swelled the grain and for the sun that ripened
it. Thank You for the people who worked so
hard to plant the seed, for those who harvested
the crop and for all who were involved so that
I can sit here, right now, and eat this bread.

Lord, I pray for the land where the rain hasn't fallen, for those who don't have food to eat today. Give them today their daily bread. Please enable the aid workers to get food to the people. And, Lord, help me to share what I have.

» » » »

A bee buzzes around the wood sorrel. These flowers are so beautiful, so delicate, such fine markings. Look, that one still has dew drops on it. Lord, they are just lovely. Thank You.

Out into the open countryside: forget-me-nots, shy little violets, daffodils and dandelions make splashes of colour along the wayside. Even the dandelions look beautiful and their leaves and roots are medicinal too. Thank You, thank You.

Down the road and along the track, a stonewall just right
to sit on and look over to the hills. Hills, Lord, that You
created. Once probably jagged mountains but now they
have been softened and moulded over the years by blasts
of ice, wind and rain; home now to hares, grouse and
ptarmigan. Your world is full of mountains, some high,
majestic and snow-capped like the Alps, the Himalayas,
the Andes and the range upon range in Greenland.
Oh Lord, how great You are.

≫ ≫ ≫ ≫

Now, just look at these little, goblet-shaped, lichen bodies on this stone beside me. I must look closer. See, through the macro lens they look like great stone statues. I find them fascinating.

Two pink ears appear; a baby rabbit, lots of rabbits. Thud! Thumper is sounding the alarm. White tails bob. Grey bodies streak. Not a rabbit in sight. It's amazing how the animals and birds warn one another of danger.

Back up via the field to the wood again. Riders on horseback appear, the sun catching their bright clothes. What beautiful horses! Kings used to go to battle on horses. Lord, You rode a donkey, a humble donkey. The King of Glory, the Lord of Creation, riding a donkey. Lord, I am so proud at times. Help me to be humble. Oh Lord, how great You are. My heart just wells up in worship.

"I will praise God's name in song and glorify him with thanksgiving."

Psalm 69 : 30

A child paused in his playing. With head thrown back, his eyes searched higher and higher as he gazed with wonder at the mighty cascade of water crashing over the rocks in relentless splendour.

The father watched, smiling at the boy stilled for a moment by his sense of awe. The mother, if that was his mother, seemed to be thinking of other things.

The scene caught my eye recently. I too enjoyed the little boy's wonder at something so great. Then, as he ran off, I went and stood where he had stood. I gazed at and listened to the amazing, ever-changing, force of life pouring out into the pool below.

I think of the awesome vision of Jesus that the apostle John had, when he was imprisoned on the isle of Patmos. He wrote:

"... and his voice sounded like the roar of a waterfall."
Revelation 1:15 CEV

Lord, how powerful and life-giving is Your Word.

Sometimes it can feel as though God has left us in a heap, just like these nets. However, for those who trust in God, for those who are His, His promise is that He will never leave nor forsake us. Jesus promises to be with us until the end.

At a time when I felt that God had forgotten me and I communicated this to Him, the answer came swiftly:

"Can a mother forget the baby at her breast and have no compassion on the child she has borne? Though she may forget, I will not forget you! See, I have engraved you on the palms of my hands; ..."

Isaiah 49:15-16

It is not in His character to abandon us. He is the Good Shepherd who goes after the sheep that is lost. Our remit is to trust and to surrender our lives to Him.

"... Never will I leave you; never will I forsake you."

Hebrews 13:5

The Amplified Bible for Hebrews 13:5 really underlines this promise:

"... for He [God] Himself has said, I will not in any way fail you nor give you up nor leave you without support. [I will] not, [I will] not, [I will] not in any degree leave you helpless nor forsake nor let [you] down (relax My hold on you)! [Assuredly not!]"

The old anchor lay ashore,
no longer able to hold fast
those once dependent on it.
Another anchor now must be
the stay in stormy blast.

There is an old hymn which goes like this:

Will your anchor hold in the storms of life,
When the clouds unfold their wings of strife?
When the strong tides lift, and the cables strain,
Will your anchor drift, or firm remain?

We have an anchor that keeps the soul
Steadfast and sure while the billows roll,
Fastened to the Rock which cannot move,
Grounded firm and deep in the Saviour's love.

We cannot always avoid the stormy blasts that
rock our boat but there is an anchor available
that will hold us fast. Is it this anchor we will
let down or some other?

"... We have run to God for safety. Now his promises should greatly encourage us to take hold of the hope that is right in front of us. This hope is like a firm and steady anchor for our souls. ..."

Hebrews 6:18-19 CEV

Built centuries ago, this harbour wall still stands, sturdily fending off the fury of the sea. Within the shelter of its walls is a quiet haven.

Whether harbour wall, broch or bothy, walls can bring a sense of safety, a shelter from the elements or the enemy.

King David often spoke about God as his refuge, fortress or strong tower; and so He can be for us too.

Sometimes, however, there are walls that cause us to feel hemmed in or shut out. When I look at the steps in the photograph opposite, they make me think of the ladder of praise and prayer that connects us with heaven. Praise takes us to a higher level. Jacob saw angels coming down and going up a ladder. Prayer summons help and passes through all walls. When Jeremiah was shut up within prison walls, God said to him:

"Call to Me, and I will answer you, and show you great and mighty things, which you do not know."

Jeremiah 33:3 NKJV

An upturned, red-bottomed boat made a lovely splash of colour high on the beach. As I lifted my camera, I noticed the very small window in the gable end of the house. I'm never quite sure why I like little windows such as these, but sometimes I wonder:

What lies behind
that little window in the wall?
A safe place in a storm,
snug from the pelting rain?
Or is there someone in there looking out,
frustrated by a narrow view?

I'm glad at least the little window's there
for sunbeams will come through.

True words from Heaven,
like shafts of light, can suddenly make clear
things hitherto unseen.
And in a moment may reveal the Door,
the Way into the light.

"The entrance of Your words gives light; ..."
Psalm 119:130 NKJV

43

" Oh, send out Your light and Your truth!
Let them lead me ..." Psalm 43:3 NKJV

Almost encompassed by light,
a couple pause. They linger,
fascinated by something in
the receding waters. I often wish I had gone
to see what it was they were looking at.
But as that great expanse of light surrounded
us with a dazzling clarity, I seemed held
somewhere between earth and heaven.
Though not possible to capture adequately
on camera, it was a moment that is etched
indelibly on my mind.

Recently, I was in another country where
I experienced heat, noise, dirt, danger and
discomfort that, for a while, just had to be
endured. Into my mind came words that were
penned from the discomfort of a Roman prison:

"... whatever is true, ... noble, ... right, ... pure, ...
lovely, ... admirable, ... excellent or praiseworthy-
think about such things. ... And the God of
peace will be with you." Philippians 4:8-9

Although it may not be quite the sort of thing that Paul had in mind, it was to this scene that my mind went. All the discomfort fell away as it was overcome by the remembrance of that amazing light.

A number of insects were avidly feasting on the Viper's Bugloss flower, including the brightly spotted Burnet moths. Then suddenly, to my great delight, a butterfly alighted. That was a bonus indeed!

Recently, watching a beautiful Peacock butterfly spreading its wings as it fed, I was reminded that butterflies need to expose their wings to the warmth of the sun to be able to fly. How often am I 'grounded', I wonder, simply because I do not expose my mind and heart to God as I feed on His word?

The butterfly came back again and again to drink the nectar. God is always ready to give us more. The warmth of His presence and the 'food' that He provides will give us all the strength we need for gaining new heights in our lives. Who knows to what far places He might take us (literally or metaphorically).

Apparently, when the Monarch butterfly migrates, it travels an amazing 3,000 miles to a place it has never been before.

"… 'My Presence will go with you, and I will give you rest.' Then Moses said to him, 'If your Presence does not go with us, do not send us up from here.'"

Exodus 33:14-15

While blowing sand is not the best conditions for a camera, the wonderful texture of these rocks was too great to miss. The glowing, fractured pyramid bore testimony to the power of sand and sea.

I love watching sand being blown across the beach. Apparently, the wind blowing onto sand first lifts one grain of sand, which, when it lands a bit farther on, causes two or three grains to be lifted. These in turn cause several more to be caught up. Eventually a sand dune is formed and in time, the whole landscape is changed.

Lord, let me be a grain of sand, lifted by the wind of your Spirit, helping to sculpt and change the landscape of lives into something lovely.

Thousands diving,
calling, crying,
jostling, fighting,
nesting.

Leave me
on my own awhile,
just to bob about and 'be'.

Gently swimming close to shore,
I see what others do not see.

Someone's watching... waiting...
quietly calling,
'You're so special';
just for me.

So Special

After another disappointment of not being able to go out
to the gannet colony because of the weather, we wandered
over to the sea wall. There, bobbing about in the water, was
a beautiful gannet. It was all alone. The Bass Rock was
seething with 150,000 others, making this one seem
like a special gift.

If we belong to Christ we are special to Him so remember,
'Someone's watching, waiting, quietly calling ...'

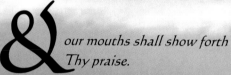

*& our mouths shall show forth
Thy praise.*

Response at Evensong

Are these random notes that string across
the evening sky less meaningful than those
we sing?

I wonder, are my words just reminiscent of
true praise or do I really have a love song
in my heart?

Pondering this, I determined to sing a song to
Him that night that was just from me. I made up
my own words and, as I sang in my heart, there
seemed to come an added harmony from somewhere.
A new joy flooded me. I think He had heard!

What about my life song? Do the notes of what I do
or say make jarring sounds or twitter like a swallow
(Isaiah 38:14)? Or is there a melody in the air with
notes that ring both clear and true, rich and deep?

Will my mouth 'show forth' His praise - even in
difficult circumstances? A challenging thought!

There in the field below,
like nails set out for a giant carpenter,
hay roll shadows pierce the stubble
burnished by the evening sun.

Morning sun had seen them facing west
but, fickle-like, they changed allegiance.
Shifting, shrinking, reappearing,
briefly now they've nailed their colours
to the east.

We may be fickle at times in our love for God, but
He never changes.

"*Every good and perfect gift is from above, coming down from the Father of the heavenly lights, who does not change like shifting shadows.*" James 1 : 17

As I walked through the dew-drenched field, a fragrance arose that was fresh and lovely. From every blade of grass, moss capsule and spider's web, droplets of dew hung like splendid pearls. Gently and refreshingly the dew had fallen.

Some pine needles and moss on a wall provided me with these photographs without having to go to extreme measures. But for a certain beetle in the desert, dew is so vital that it will even stand on its head, so that dewdrops forming on its body will run down into its mouth. Other times it exposes its abdomen to collect the precious moisture.

So it is, as we expose ourselves to God's word, the dew falls, and blessing and refreshment follow.

Moses said, *"Let my teaching fall like rain and my words descend like dew ..."* Deuteronomy 32:2

Isaac blessed his sons with, *"the dew of heaven"*. Genesis 27:28 NKJV

For all who read this book, I pray blessing
and refreshment.

May God give you of heaven's dew.

Pat Lomax

Sometimes it can feel as though God has left us in a heap, just like these nets. However, for those who trust in God, for those who are His, His promise is that He will never leave nor forsake us. Jesus promises to be with us until the end.

At a time when I felt that God had forgotten me and I communicated this to Him, the answer came swiftly:

"Can a mother forget the baby at her breast and have no compassion on the child she has borne? Though she may forget, I will not forget you! See, I have engraved you on the palms of my hands; ..."

Isaiah 49:15-16

It is not in His character to abandon us. He is the Good Shepherd who goes after the sheep that is lost. Our remit is to trust and to surrender our lives to Him.

"... Never will I leave you; never will I forsake you."

Hebrews 13:5